FAVORITE BRAND NAME RECIPES

JELL-O®

BRAND

Celebrating 100 Years

PUBLICATIONS INTERNATIONAL, LTD.

EH

Desserts & Snacks Division Promotion Manager: Jeany Mui
Kraft Creative Kitchens Division Manager: Debra-Ann Robinson
Kraft Creative Kitchens Consumer Foods Associate: Mary Lee-Brody
Contributing Writer: Hunter & Associates, Inc., New York, NY

Photography: Sacco Productions Limited, Chicago
Photographers: Marc A. Frisco, Mike McKenzie
Photo Stylist: Melissa J. Frisco
Food Stylists: Amy Andrews, Gail O'Donnell, Bonnie Rabert, Teri Rys-Maki
Assistant Food Stylists: Kim Hartman, Susie Skoog

Pictured on the front cover: Cranberry Fruit Mold *(page 82)*.

Pictured on the back cover *(clockwise from top left):* Striped Delight *(page 46)*, Layered Pear Cream Cheese Mold *(page 22)*, Sand Cups and Dirt Cups *(page 38)*, COOL 'N EASY® Pie *(page 56)*.

ISBN: 0-7853-2300-7

Manufactured in U.S.A.

8 7 6 5 4 3 2 1

 Nutrition Information: We've provided nutrition information for some of the recipes in this publication, as now more than ever, people are interested in nutrition and health. These recipes will help you keep an eye on eating right without giving up food favorites or sacrificing taste for good nutrition. Remember, eating can be both healthy and enjoyable.

Microwave Cooking: Microwave ovens vary in wattage. Use the cooking times as guidelines and check for doneness before adding more time.

Preparation/Cooking Times: Preparation times are based on the approximate amount of time required to assemble the recipe before cooking, baking, chilling or serving. These times include preparation steps such as measuring, chopping and mixing. The fact that some preparations and cooking can be done simultaneously is taken into account. Preparation of optional ingredients and serving suggestions is not included.

JELL-O®

BRAND

Celebrating 100 Years

8.99

After 100 Years...
Still The Coolest™!

Looking back 100 years ago, Jell-O was little more than a brand name and an unfulfilled dream.

Today, if placed end to end, the 299 million packages of Jell-O gelatin dessert produced in a year would stretch more than three fifths of the way around the globe. And the Jell-O brand now includes extensive lines of pudding mixes, No Bakes, snacks and yogurts—fun products which meet the needs of families today.

How did this phenomenon come about? How has this wiggly, jiggly product adapted to changes in lifestyles and eating habits to remain a brand recognized by 99% of Americans and used regularly in 72% of our homes?

Actually, the Jell-O story began more than 150 years ago in LeRoy, New York. In 1845, the industrialist, inventor and philanthropist Peter Cooper, of Tom Thumb engine and Cooper Union fame, obtained the first patent for a gelatin dessert.

Although he packaged his gelatin in neat little boxes with directions for use, Cooper did very little to make the product more convenient to use. Home cooks still relied on sheets of prepared gelatin. These sheets had to be clarified by boiling them with egg whites and shells and then dripped through a jelly bag before they could be turned into shimmering molds.

Today Jell-O products are not only the largest selling prepared desserts, but the brand is one of the best known in the whole field of grocery products. Its history through the years has been one of adapting to contemporary consumer needs and desires, and it continues to do so. The brand is a popular and familiar icon. In addition to a restaurant and museum devoted to Jell-O, there are Jell-O fans and memorabilia collectors all over the country. Now there is even a Jell-O home page on the Kraft Foods, Inc. Web site at http://www.kraftfoods.com.

Over 100 varieties of snacks and desserts are sold under the Jell-O brand. In the United States, every eight seconds someone buys a package of Jell-O gelatin, the dessert from LeRoy, New York, that started it all 100 years ago. We invite you to page through this spectacular collection of Jell-O recipes for dozens of ideas sure to please one and all. Enjoy!

Tips & Techniques

All of the recipes appearing in this publication have been developed and tested by the food professionals in the JELL-O Test Kitchens to ensure your success in making them. We also share our JELL-O secrets with you. These foolproof tips, many with step-by-step photos, help you get perfect results every time.

GELATIN

Making JELL-O Brand Gelatin Dessert is easy. Just follow the package directions and the results will be a success.

The basic directions as written below are also on the package:

• Stir 1 cup boiling water into 1 package (4-serving size) gelatin at least 2 minutes until completely dissolved. Stir in 1 cup cold water. Refrigerate 4 hours or until firm. (For an 8-serving size package, use 2 cups boiling water and 2 cups cold water.)

• JELL-O Brand Sugar Free Low Calorie Gelatin Dessert is prepared in the same way. It can be used in many recipes that call for JELL-O Brand Gelatin Dessert.

Some tips for success

• To make a mixture that is clear and uniformly set, be sure the gelatin is completely dissolved in boiling water or other boiling liquid before adding the cold water.

• To double a recipe, just double the amounts of gelatin, liquid and other ingredients used, except salt, vinegar and lemon juice. For these, use 1½ times the amount given in the recipe.

• To store prepared gelatin overnight or longer, cover it before refrigerating to prevent drying. Always store gelatin desserts and molds in the refrigerator.

• Generally, gelatin molds are best served right from the refrigerator. A gelatin mold containing fruit or vegetables can remain at room temperature up to 2 hours. Always keep a gelatin mold containing meat, mayonnaise, ice cream or other dairy products refrigerated until ready to serve. Also, do not let it sit at room temperature longer than 30 minutes. Store any leftover gelatin mold in the refrigerator.

How to Speed Up Refrigerating Time

• Choose the right container. Use a metal bowl or mold rather than glass, plastic or china. Metal chills more quickly and the gelatin will be firm in less time than in glass or plastic bowls.

• Use the speed set (ice cube) method. (Do not use this method if you are going to mold gelatin.) For a 4-serving size package, stir ¾ cup boiling water into gelatin in medium bowl at least 2 minutes until completely dissolved. Mix ½ cup cold water and ice cubes to make 1¼ cups. Add to gelatin, stirring until slightly thickened. Remove any remaining ice. Refrigerate 30 minutes for a soft set or 1 to 1½ hours until firm. (For an 8-serving size package, use 1½ cups boiling water. Mix 1 cup cold water and ice cubes to make 2½ cups.)

- Use the ice bath method. (This method will speed up the preparation of layered gelatin molds.) Prepare gelatin as directed on package. Place bowl of gelatin in a larger bowl of ice and water. Stir occasionally as mixture chills to ensure even thickening.

- Use the blender method. (This method can be used to make quick and easy layered gelatin desserts.) Place 1 package (4-serving size) gelatin and ¾ cup boiling liquid in blender container; cover. Blend on low speed 30 seconds. Mix ½ cup cold water and ice cubes to make 1¼ cups. Add to gelatin, stirring until partially melted; cover. Blend on low speed 30 seconds. Pour into dessert dishes. Refrigerate at least 30 minutes or until set. The mixture sets with a frothy layer on top and a clear layer on bottom. (Use this method for 4-serving size package only. The volume of liquid required for an 8-serving size package is too large for most blenders.)

Gelatin Refrigerating Time Chart

In all recipes, for best results, the gelatin needs to be refrigerated to the proper consistency. Use this chart as a guideline to determine the desired consistency and the approximate refrigerating time.

When a recipe says:	It means gelatin should:	Refrigerating Time:		Gelatin Uses:
		Regular set	Speed set*	
"Refrigerate until syrupy"	Be consistency of thick syrup	1 hour	3 minutes	Glaze for pies, fruit
"Refrigerate until slightly thickened"	Be consistency of unbeaten egg whites	1¼ hours	5 to 6 minutes	Adding creamy ingredients or when mixture will be beaten
"Refrigerate until thickened"	Be thick enough so that a spoon drawn through leaves a definite impression	1½ hours	7 to 8 minutes	Adding solid ingredients such as fruits or vegetables
"Refrigerate until set but not firm"	Stick to finger when touched and should mound or move to the side when bowl or mold is tilted	2 hours	30 minutes	Layering gelatin mixtures
"Refrigerate until firm"	Not stick to finger when touched and not mound or move when mold is tilted	Individual molds: at least 3 hours 2- to 6-cup mold: at least 4 hours 8- to 12-cup mold: at least 5 hours or overnight		Unmolding and serving

Speed set (ice cube) method is not recommended for molding.

Gelatin Consistencies

Gelatin should be consistency of thick syrup.

Set but not firm gelatin should stick to finger when touched and should mound or move to the side when bowl or mold is tilted.

Slightly thickened gelatin should be consistency of unbeaten egg whites.

Firm gelatin should not stick to finger when touched and should not move when mold is tilted.

Thickened gelatin should be thick enough so that a spoon drawn through it leaves a definite inpression.

The Secret to Molding Gelatin

The Mold

• Use metal molds, traditional decorative molds and other metal forms, or plastic molds. You can use square or round cake pans, fluted or plain tube pans, loaf pans, or metal mixing bowls (the nested sets give you a variety of sizes). You can also use metal fruit or juice cans. (To unmold, dip can in warm water, then puncture bottom of can and unmold.)

• To determine the volume of the mold, measure first with water. Most recipes give an indication of the size of the mold needed. For clear gelatin, you need a 2-cup mold for a 4-serving size package and a 4-cup mold for an 8-serving size package.

• If mold holds less than the size called for, pour the extra gelatin into a separate dish. Refrigerate and serve it at another time. Do not use a mold that is too large, since it would be difficult to unmold. Either increase the recipe or use a smaller mold.

• For easier unmolding, spray mold with no stick cooking spray before filling mold.

The Preparation

• To prepare gelatin for molding, use less water than the amount called for on the package. For a 4-serving size package, decrease cold water to ¾ cup. For an 8-serving size package, decrease cold water to 1½ cups. (This adjustment has already been made in the recipes in this publication.) The firmer consistency will result in a less fragile mold. It also makes unmolding much simpler.

• To arrange fruits or vegetables in the mold, refrigerate gelatin until thickened. (If gelatin is not thick enough, fruits or vegetables may sink or float.) Pour gelatin into mold to about ¼-inch depth. Reserve remaining gelatin at room temperature. Arrange fruits or vegetables in decorative pattern on gelatin. Refrigerate mold until gelatin is set but not firm. Spoon reserved gelatin over pattern in mold. Refrigerate until firm, then unmold.

The Unmolding

• First, allow gelatin to set until firm by refrigerating several hours or overnight. Also chill serving plate on which mold is to be served by storing in refrigerator.

• Make certain that gelatin is completely firm. It should not feel sticky on top and should not mound or move to the side if mold is tilted.

• Moisten tips of fingers and gently pull gelatin from around edge of mold. Or, use a small metal spatula or pointed knife dipped in warm water to loosen top edge.

• Dip mold in warm, not hot, water just to rim for about 15 seconds. Lift from water, hold upright and shake to loosen gelatin. Or, gently pull gelatin from edge of mold.

• Moisten chilled serving plate with water. (This allows gelatin to be moved after unmolding.) Place moistened serving plate on top of mold. Invert mold and plate; holding mold and plate together, shake slightly to loosen. Gently remove mold. If gelatin does not release easily, dip mold in warm water again for a few seconds. Center gelatin on serving plate.

Unmolding

1. Before unmolding, gently pull gelatin from around edge of mold with moist fingertips.

4. Place moistened serving plate on top of mold.

2. Dip mold in warm water, just to the rim, for about 15 seconds.

5. Invert mold and plate; shake to loosen gelatin.

3. Lift mold from water, hold upright and shake to loosen gelatin.

6. Remove mold and center gelatin on plate.

Simple Additions

Fruits and Vegetables

- Refrigerate gelatin until thickened. For a 4-serving size package, add ¾ to 1½ cups sliced or chopped fruit or vegetables. (For an 8-serving size package, add 1½ to 3 cups.) Do not use fresh or frozen pineapple, kiwi, gingerroot, papaya, figs or guava. An enzyme in these fruits will prevent the gelatin from setting. However, if cooked or canned, these fruits may be used. Drain canned or fresh fruits well before adding to the gelatin (unless a recipe specifies otherwise). The fruit juice or syrup can be used to replace part of the cold water used in preparing the gelatin.

- Some favorite fresh fruits include apples, bananas, peaches, oranges, grapefruit, melons, grapes, pears, strawberries, blueberries and raspberries. Canned fruits include peaches, pineapple, pears, apricots, mandarin oranges, cherries and fruit cocktail. Dried fruits, such as raisins, currants, figs, dates, apricots or prunes, can be added to gelatin. Nuts, such as coconut, walnuts, pecans and almonds, can also be used.

- Gelatin salads can include fresh vegetables, such as carrots, celery, peppers, onions, cucumbers, tomatoes or summer squash. Serve them on crisp salad greens.

Carbonated Beverages

Substitute cold carbonated beverages, such as seltzer, club soda, fruit-flavored seltzer, ginger ale or a lemon-lime carbonated beverage, for part or all of the cold water. (Do not use tonic water.)

Fruit Juice or Iced Tea

Use fruit juices, such as orange, apple, cranberry, canned pineapple or white grape juice, for part of the cold water. Nectars, such as apricot, peach and mango, or juice blends and drinks can also be substituted. Or, use iced tea, plain or flavored, for part of the cold water.

Citrus Fruits

Adding grated orange, lemon or lime peel and lemon or lime juice will add zing to your gelatin. Add 1 teaspoon grated peel and/or 1 tablespoon juice to a 4-serving size package of gelatin. For an 8-serving size package, use 1½ teaspoons grated peel and 1½ tablespoons juice.

Flavored Extracts

Add just a touch of flavoring extracts, such as vanilla, almond, peppermint or rum, for additional flavor.

PUDDING

The recipes in this publication use both JELL-O Cook & Serve Pudding & Pie Filling, which requires cooking, and JELL-O Instant Pudding & Pie Filling, which is not cooked. These products are not interchangeable in recipes. Be sure to use the product called for in the recipe.

JELL-O Instant Pudding & Pie Filling is also available Fat Free. Both the Instant and the Cook & Serve Pudding & Pie Fillings are also available as Sugar Free Fat Free.

See individual packages for basic directions for preparing the products as either a pudding or a pie filling.

Some Tips for Success

For JELL-O Instant Pudding & Pie Filling

- Always use cold milk. Beat pudding mix slowly, not vigorously.

- For best results, use 2% lowfat milk or whole milk. Skim, 1% lowfat, reconstituted nonfat dry milk or lactose-reduced milk can also be used. For Fat Free or Sugar Free Fat Free Pudding & Pie Filling, use cold skim milk.

- Always store prepared pudding desserts, pies and snacks in the refrigerator.

For JELL-O Cook & Serve Pudding & Pie Filling

- It's best to cook the pudding in a heavy saucepan to ensure even heating. Stir pudding mixture constantly as it cooks. Make sure it comes to full boil. The mixture will be thin, but will thicken as it cools.

- For a creamier pudding, place a piece of plastic wrap on the surface of pudding while cooling. Stir before serving.

- To cool pudding quickly, place saucepan of hot pudding in larger pan of ice water; stir frequently until mixture is cooled. Do not use this method for pie filling.

Simple Additions

- Stir mix-ins such as chopped candy bar, chopped cookies, candy-coated milk chocolate candies, peanut butter or butterscotch chips, BAKER'S Semi-Sweet Real Chocolate Chips, miniature marshmallows, nuts or toasted BAKER'S ANGEL FLAKE Coconut into prepared pudding just before serving.

- Stir fruit such as chopped banana or strawberries, raspberries, blueberries, mandarin orange segments or drained canned fruit cocktail into prepared pudding just before serving.

- For spiced pudding, stir ½ teaspoon ground cinnamon into a 4-serving size package of pudding mix before adding cold milk.

NO BAKE CHEESECAKES and DESSERTS

Some Tips for Success

- The cheesecake can also be prepared in an 8- or 9-inch square pan or 12 foil- or paper-lined muffin cups.

- Two packages of the cheesecake can be prepared in a 13×9-inch pan or a 9×3-inch springform pan.

- To serve, dip the pie plate just to the rim in hot water for 30 seconds before cutting.

- To freeze, cover the cheesecake. Freeze up to 2 weeks. Thaw in refrigerator 3 hours before serving.

- For easy cleanup, line the 8- or 9-inch square pan with foil before preparing the No Bake Dessert.

- The No Bake Desserts can also be served frozen. Freeze 4 hours or until firm. Remove from freezer and serve immediately.

Shimmering Molds

Cucumber Sour Cream Mold

Complement poached salmon or shrimp with this refreshingly cool molded salad.

> 1½ cups boiling water
> 1 package (8-serving size) or 2 packages (4-serving size)
>   JELL-O Brand Lime Flavor Gelatin Dessert
> ¼ teaspoon salt
> 1½ cups cold water
> 1 tablespoon lemon juice
> ½ cup MIRACLE WHIP Salad Dressing
> ½ cup BREAKSTONE'S Sour Cream
> 1½ cups chopped seeded, peeled cucumber
> 2 tablespoons minced onion
> 1 teaspoon dill weed

STIR boiling water into gelatin and salt in large bowl at least 2 minutes until completely dissolved. Stir in cold water and lemon juice. Refrigerate about 1¼ hours or until slightly thickened (consistency of unbeaten egg whites).

MIX salad dressing and sour cream in small bowl until well blended. Stir into thickened gelatin. Refrigerate about 15 minutes or until thickened (spoon drawn through leaves definite impression). Stir in cucumbers, onion and dill weed. Pour into 5-cup mold.

REFRIGERATE 4 hours or until firm. Unmold. Garnish as desired.

Makes 10 servings

Preparation Time: 15 minutes
Refrigerating Time: 5½ hours

15

Top to bottom: Cranberry Cream Cheese Mold (page 16), Sunset Fruit Salad (page 26), White Sangria Splash (page 17), Cucumber Sour Cream Mold

Cranberry Cream Cheese Mold

Piquant cranberry flavor is one of the hits of the 1990's. Now you no longer have to save it just for the Thanksgiving holiday.

Add sparkle to your festive buffet with this dramatic double-layer fruit mold.

1½ cups boiling water
1 package (8-serving size) or 2 packages (4-serving size) JELL-O Brand Cranberry Flavor Gelatin Dessert, or any red flavor
1½ cups cold water
½ teaspoon ground cinnamon
1 medium apple, chopped
1 cup whole berry cranberry sauce
1 package (8 ounces) PHILADELPHIA BRAND Cream Cheese, softened

STIR boiling water into gelatin in large bowl at least 2 minutes until completely dissolved. Stir in cold water and cinnamon. Reserve 1 cup gelatin at room temperature. Refrigerate remaining gelatin about 1½ hours or until thickened (spoon drawn through leaves definite impression).

STIR apple and cranberry sauce into thickened gelatin. Spoon into 6-cup mold. Refrigerate about 30 minutes or until set but not firm (gelatin should stick to finger when touched and should mound).

STIR reserved 1 cup gelatin gradually into cream cheese in medium bowl with wire whisk until smooth. Pour over gelatin layer in mold.

REFRIGERATE 4 hours or until firm. Unmold. Garnish as desired.   *Makes 12 servings*

Note: *To prepare without cream cheese layer, omit cream cheese. Refrigerate all of the gelatin about 1½ hours or until thickened. Stir in apple and cranberry sauce. Pour into mold. Refrigerate.*

Preparation Time: 20 minutes
Refrigerating Time: 6 hours

White Sangria Splash

Wine adds the right touch to this fruity dessert.

> 1 cup dry white wine
> 1 package (8-serving size) or 2 packages
>   (4-serving size) JELL-O Brand Lemon
>   Flavor Sugar Free Low Calorie Gelatin
>   Dessert or JELL-O Brand Lemon Flavor
>   Gelatin Dessert
> 3 cups cold seltzer or club soda
> 1 tablespoon lime juice
> 1 tablespoon orange juice or orange liqueur
> 3 cups seedless grapes, divided
> 1 cup sliced strawberries
> 1 cup whole small strawberries

Gelatin desserts made with wine have long been favorites for elegant entertaining. They are easy to make and impressive to serve. JELL-O gelatin can even trap the bubbles from champagne.

BRING wine to boil in small saucepan. Stir boiling wine into gelatin in medium bowl at least 2 minutes until completely dissolved. Stir in cold seltzer and lime and orange juices. Place bowl of gelatin in larger bowl of ice and water. Let stand about 10 minutes or until thickened (spoon drawn through leaves definite impression), stirring occasionally.

STIR in 1 cup of the grapes and the sliced strawberries. Pour into 6-cup mold.

REFRIGERATE 4 hours or until firm. Unmold. Garnish with remaining grapes and whole strawberries.   *Makes 12 servings*

Nutrition Information Per Serving (using JELL-O Brand Lemon Flavor Sugar Free Low Calorie Gelatin Dessert and orange juice): *60 calories, 0g fat, 0mg cholesterol, 55mg sodium, 9g carbohydrate, 1g dietary fiber, 9g sugars, 1g protein, 35% daily value vitamin C*

Preparation Time: 15 minutes
Refrigerating Time: 4 hours

Gazpacho Salad

This jazzed-up variation on tomato aspic adopts the flavor and texture of the famous Spanish cold soup.

Enjoy the taste of Spain with this fat free tangy salad.

  1 cup diced tomato
  ½ cup diced peeled cucumber
  ¼ cup diced green pepper
  2 tablespoons diced red pepper
  2 tablespoons thinly sliced green onion
  2 tablespoons vinegar
  ¼ teaspoon pepper
  ⅛ teaspoon garlic powder (optional)
1½ cups tomato juice
  1 package (4-serving size) JELL-O Brand Lemon Flavor Sugar Free Low Calorie Gelatin Dessert or JELL-O Brand Lemon Flavor Gelatin Dessert
  Crackers (optional)

MIX vegetables, vinegar, pepper and garlic powder in medium bowl; set aside. Bring tomato juice to boil in small saucepan. Stir into gelatin in large bowl at least 2 minutes until completely dissolved. Refrigerate about 1¼ hours or until slightly thickened (consistency of unbeaten egg whites).

STIR in vegetable mixture. Pour into 4-cup mold.

REFRIGERATE 3 hours or until firm. Unmold. Serve with crackers if desired. Garnish as desired.

Makes 6 servings

Nutrition Information Per Serving (using JELL-O Brand Lemon Flavor Sugar Free Low Calorie Gelatin Dessert and omitting crackers and garnish): *30 calories, 0g fat, 0mg cholesterol, 260mg sodium, 5g carbohydrate, less than 1g dietary fiber, 4g sugars, 2g protein, 15% daily value vitamin A, 50% daily value vitamin C*

Preparation Time: 20 minutes
Refrigerating Time: 4¼ hours

Gazpacho Salad

19

Creamy Fruited Mold

Fluffy and delicious!

> 1 cup boiling water
> 1 package (4-serving size) JELL-O
>   Brand Gelatin Dessert, any flavor
> 1 cup cold water or apple juice
> 2½ cups thawed COOL WHIP Whipped
>   Topping
> 1 cup diced fruit

STIR boiling water into gelatin in medium bowl at least 2 minutes until completely dissolved. Stir in cold water. Refrigerate about 1¼ hours or until slightly thickened (consistency of unbeaten egg whites). Gently stir in whipped topping. Refrigerate about 15 minutes or until thickened (spoon drawn through leaves definite impression). Stir in fruit. Pour into 5-cup mold.

REFRIGERATE 4 hours or until firm. Unmold. Garnish as desired.

Makes 8 servings

Preparation Time: 15 minutes
Refrigerating Time: 5½ hours

1911

20

21

Creamy Fruited Mold

Layered Pear Cream Cheese Mold

Guests will enjoy this beautiful emerald-topped mold flavored with a hint of ginger.

Carbonated beverages add pizzazz to molded gelatin salads. Club soda, fruit-flavored sparkling water, ginger ale or lemon-lime flavored drinks can be substituted for all or part of the cold water.

1 can (16 ounces) pear halves, undrained
1 package (8-serving size) or 2 packages (4-serving size) JELL-O Brand Lime Flavor Gelatin Dessert
1½ cups cold ginger ale or water
2 tablespoons lemon juice
1 package (8 ounces) PHILADELPHIA BRAND Cream Cheese, softened
¼ cup chopped pecans

DRAIN pears, reserving liquid. Dice pears; set aside. Add water to liquid to make 1½ cups; bring to boil in small saucepan.

STIR boiling liquid into gelatin in large bowl at least 2 minutes until completely dissolved. Stir in cold ginger ale and lemon juice. Reserve 2½ cups gelatin at room temperature. Pour remaining gelatin into 5-cup mold. Refrigerate about 30 minutes or until thickened (spoon drawn through leaves definite impression). Arrange about ½ cup of the diced pears in thickened gelatin in mold.

STIR reserved 2½ cups gelatin gradually into cream cheese in large bowl with wire whisk until smooth. Refrigerate about 30 minutes or until slightly thickened (consistency of unbeaten egg whites). Stir in remaining diced pears and pecans. Spoon over gelatin layer in mold.

REFRIGERATE 4 hours or until firm. Unmold. Garnish as desired.   *Makes 10 servings*

Preparation Time: 30 minutes
Refrigerating Time: 5 hours

Layered Pear Cream Cheese Mold

Sparkling Berry Salad

Fruit should be added to gelatin that has been chilled until it thickens, but is not yet set. This way, the fruit remains suspended in the gelatin.

Capture the freshness of spring with this fat free berry-filled mold.

2 cups boiling diet cranberry juice cocktail
1 package (8-serving size) or 2 packages (4-serving size) JELL-O Brand Sugar Free Low Calorie Gelatin Dessert or JELL-O Brand Gelatin Dessert, any red flavor
1½ cups cold seltzer or club soda
¼ cup creme de cassis liqueur (optional)
1 teaspoon lemon juice
3 cups assorted berries (blueberries, raspberries and sliced strawberries), divided

STIR boiling cranberry juice into gelatin in large bowl at least 2 minutes until completely dissolved. Stir in cold seltzer, liqueur and lemon juice. Refrigerate about 1½ hours or until thickened (spoon drawn through leaves definite impression).

STIR in 2 cups of the berries. Spoon into 5-cup mold.

REFRIGERATE 4 hours or until firm. Unmold. Top with remaining 1 cup berries.

Makes 8 servings

Nutrition Information Per Serving (using JELL-O Brand Sugar Free Low Calorie Gelatin Dessert, liqueur and 1 cup each blueberries, raspberries and strawberries): *70 calories, 0g fat, 0mg cholesterol, 95mg sodium, 12g carbohydrate, 2g dietary fiber, 10g sugars, 2g protein, 50% daily value vitamin C*

Preparation Time: 15 minutes
Refrigerating Time: 5½ hours

25

Sparkling Berry Salad

Sunset Fruit Salad

This spectacular fat free salad reflects the colors of the setting sun.

This recipe was first created in 1931, when molded gelatin salads were at the height of their popularity. At that time, almost one third of the salad recipes in the average cookbook were gelatin-based.

2 cups boiling water
1 package (4-serving size) JELL-O Brand Cranberry Flavor Sugar Free Low Calorie Gelatin Dessert or JELL-O Brand Cranberry Flavor Gelatin Dessert, or any red flavor
½ cup cold water
1 can (8 ounces) sliced peaches in juice, drained, chopped
1 package (4-serving size) JELL-O Brand Orange Flavor Sugar Free Low Calorie Gelatin Dessert or JELL-O Brand Orange Flavor Gelatin Dessert
1 can (8 ounces) crushed pineapple in juice, undrained

STIR 1 cup of the boiling water into cranberry gelatin in medium bowl at least 2 minutes until completely dissolved. Stir in cold water. Refrigerate about 45 minutes or until slightly thickened (consistency of unbeaten egg whites). Stir in peaches. Spoon into 5-cup mold. Refrigerate about 15 minutes or until set but not firm (gelatin should stick to finger when touched and should mound).

MEANWHILE, stir remaining 1 cup boiling water into orange gelatin in medium bowl at least 2 minutes until completely dissolved. Stir in pineapple with juice. Pour over gelatin layer in mold.

REFRIGERATE 4 hours or until firm. Unmold. Garnish as desired.   *Makes 10 servings*

Nutrition Information Per Serving (using JELL-O Brand Cranberry and Orange Flavors Sugar Free Low Calorie Gelatin Dessert and omitting garnish): 30 calories, 0g fat, 0mg cholesterol, 60mg sodium, 6g carbohydrate, 0g dietary fiber, 7g sugars, 1g protein

Preparation Time: 20 minutes
Refrigerating Time: 5 hours

Waldorf Salad

A delectable molded version of a salad classic.

2 cups boiling water
1 package (8-serving size) or 2 packages
    (4-serving size) JELL-O Brand Lemon
    Flavor Gelatin Dessert
1 cup cold water
1 tablespoon lemon juice
½ cup KRAFT Mayo: Real Mayonnaise or
    MIRACLE WHIP Salad Dressing
1 medium red apple, diced
½ cup diced celery
¼ cup chopped walnuts
    Salad greens (optional)

The original Waldorf salad was created in the 1890's at New York's Waldorf-Astoria Hotel. It consisted of apples, celery and mayonnaise and was served on lettuce. The walnuts were added to the recipe in later years.

STIR boiling water into gelatin in large bowl at least 2 minutes until completely dissolved. Stir in cold water and lemon juice. Refrigerate about 1½ hours or until thickened (spoon drawn through leaves definite impression). Gradually stir in mayonnaise with wire whisk. Stir in apple, celery and walnuts. Pour into 5-cup mold.

REFRIGERATE 4 hours or until firm. Unmold. Serve on salad greens, if desired.

Makes 10 servings

Preparation Time: 20 minutes
Refrigerating Time: 5½ hours

JELL-O® *Fun Facts*

A 1908 ad offered a free set of six aluminum molds to JELL-O users. They were directed to buy a package of JELL-O gelatin for 10 cents to learn how to obtain the molds.

Snack Attacks

Pudding Chillers

After school is the perfect time for savoring these frozen pops.

> 2 cups cold milk
> 1 package (4-serving size) JELL-O Instant Pudding & Pie
>   Filling, any flavor
> 6 (5-ounce) paper cups

POUR milk into medium bowl. Add pudding mix. Beat with wire whisk 2 minutes. Spoon into cups. Insert wooden pop stick into each for a handle.

FREEZE 5 hours or overnight until firm. To remove pop from cup, place bottom of cup under warm running water for 15 seconds. Press firmly on bottom of cup to release pop. (Do not twist or pull pop stick.)   *Makes 6 pops*

Rocky Road: Use JELL-O Chocolate Flavor Instant Pudding & Pie Filling and stir in ½ cup miniature marshmallows and ¼ cup *each* BAKER'S Semi-Sweet Real Chocolate Chips and chopped peanuts.

Toffee Crunch: Use JELL-O Vanilla Flavor Instant Pudding & Pie Filling and stir in ½ cup chopped chocolate-covered toffee bars.

Cookies & Cream: Use JELL-O Vanilla Flavor Instant Pudding & Pie Filling and stir in ½ cup chopped chocolate sandwich cookies.

Preparation Time: 10 minutes
Freezing Time: 5 hours

Clockwise from top left: Rocky Road Pudding Chillers, Cookies & Cream Pudding Chillers, Pudding in a Cloud (page 37), JIGGLERS® (page 32), Creamy JIGGLERS® (page 32)

Refreshers

In 1991, the Smithsonian Institution held its first and only conference on JELL-O history, featuring such topics as American History is JELL-O History, JELL-O Food Wrestling, and The Dialectics of JELL-O in Peasant Culture.

1 cup boiling water
1 package (4-serving size) JELL-O Brand
    Gelatin Dessert, any flavor
1 cup cold beverage, such as seltzer, club soda,
    ginger ale, iced tea or lemon-lime
    carbonated beverage

STIR boiling water into gelatin in medium bowl at least 2 minutes until completely dissolved. Stir in cold beverage.

REFRIGERATE 4 hours or until firm. Cut into cubes and garnish as desired.   *Makes 4 servings*

Sugar Free Low Calorie Refreshers: Prepare recipe as directed above using any flavor JELL-O Brand Sugar Free Low Calorie Gelatin Dessert and 1 cup seltzer, club soda, diet ginger ale, diet iced tea or diet lemon-lime carbonated beverage.

Nutrition Information Per Serving (for Sugar Free Low Calorie Refreshers, omitting garnish): 10 calories, 0g fat, 0mg cholesterol, 90mg sodium, 0g carbohydrate, 0g dietary fiber, 0g sugars, 1g protein

Preparation Time: 5 minutes
Refrigerating Time: 4 hours

The first JELL-O flavors—strawberry, raspberry, orange and lemon—are still available today and are among the most popular flavors.

Refreshers

JIGGLERS®

Fabulous fun finger foods that kids adore!

Introduced in 1989, wiggly JELL-O JIGGLERS® is the most requested JELL-O recipe ever, according to the company's Consumer Response Center.

2½ cups boiling water or boiling apple juice (Do not add cold water or cold juice.)
2 packages (8-serving size) or 4 packages (4-serving size) JELL-O Brand Gelatin Dessert, any flavor

STIR boiling water or boiling juice into gelatin in large bowl at least 3 minutes until completely dissolved. Pour into 13×9-inch pan.

REFRIGERATE 3 hours or until firm. Dip bottom of pan in warm water about 15 seconds. Cut into decorative shapes with cookie cutters all the way through gelatin or cut into 1-inch squares. Lift from pan.   *Makes about 24 pieces*

Note: *Recipe can be halved. Use 8- or 9-inch square pan.*

Preparation Time: 10 minutes
Refrigerating Time: 3 hours

Creamy JIGGLERS®

2½ cups boiling water
2 packages (8-serving size) or 4 packages (4-serving size) JELL-O Brand Gelatin Dessert, any flavor
1 cup cold milk
1 package (4-serving size) JELL-O Vanilla Flavor Instant Pudding & Pie Filling

STIR boiling water into gelatin in large bowl at least 3 minutes until completely dissolved. Cool 30 minutes at room temperature.

POUR milk into medium bowl. Add pudding mix. Beat with wire whisk 1 minute. Quickly pour into gelatin. Stir with wire whisk until well blended. Pour into 13×9-inch pan.

REFRIGERATE 3 hours or until firm. Dip bottom of pan in warm water about 15 seconds. Cut into decorative shapes with cookie cutters all the way through gelatin or cut into 1-inch squares. Lift from pan. *Makes about 24 pieces*

Preparation Time: 15 minutes
Refrigerating Time: 3 hours

Miniature Cheesecakes

1 package (11.1 ounces) JELL-O No Bake Real
    Cheesecake
2 tablespoons sugar
⅓ cup butter or margarine, melted
1½ cups cold milk
2 squares BAKER'S Semi-Sweet Baking
    Chocolate, melted (optional)

Add a candle to each of these desserts for a quick birthday party treat.

MIX crumbs, sugar and butter thoroughly with fork in medium bowl until crumbs are well moistened. Press onto bottoms of 12 paper-lined or foil-lined muffin cups.

BEAT milk and filling mix with electric mixer on low speed until blended. Beat on medium speed 3 minutes. (Filling will be thick.) Spoon over crumb mixture in muffin cups. Drizzle with melted chocolate, if desired.

REFRIGERATE at least 1 hour or until ready to serve. Garnish as desired. *Makes 12 servings*

Preparation Time: 15 minutes
Refrigerating Time: 1 hour

33

Fruity Gelatin Pops

These super after-school treats couldn't be easier!

1 cup boiling water
1 package (4-serving size) JELL-O Brand
Gelatin Dessert, any flavor
½ cup sugar
2 cups cold water
7 (5-ounce) paper cups

STIR boiling water into gelatin and sugar in medium bowl at least 2 minutes until completely dissolved. Stir in cold water. Pour into cups. Freeze about 2 hours or until almost firm. Insert wooden pop stick into each for handle.

FREEZE 5 hours or overnight until firm. To remove pop from cup, place bottom of cup under warm running water for 15 seconds. Press firmly on bottom of cup to release pop. (Do not twist or pull pop stick.)   *Makes 7 pops*

Iced Tea Pops: Use 1 cup boiling water, JELL-O Brand Lemon Flavor Gelatin Dessert, ¼ cup sugar and 2 cups pre-sweetened iced tea.

Strawberry Pops: Use 1 cup boiling water, JELL-O Brand Strawberry Flavor Gelatin Dessert, ½ cup sugar, 1 cup cold water and 1 cup puréed strawberries.

Lemonade Pops: Use 1 cup boiling water, JELL-O Brand Lemon Flavor Gelatin Dessert, ½ cup sugar, 1¾ cups cold water and ¼ cup lemon juice.

Orange Pops: Use 1 cup boiling water, JELL-O Brand Orange Flavor Gelatin Dessert, ½ cup sugar and 2 cups orange juice.

Preparation Time: 10 minutes
Freezing Time: 7 hours

In the 1930's, JELL-O sponsored a Wizard of Oz radio program and published a series of children's booklets by Frank L. Baum. Some of the titles were: The Scarecrow and the Tin Woodman, Jack Pumpkinhead and the Sawhorse, Ozma and the Little Wizard, *and* Tiktok and the NomeKing.

Top to bottom: Lemonade Pops, Orange Pops

Fresh Fruit Parfaits

Whip up these fat free layered parfaits tonight!

Experiment with gelatin-fruit combinations such as orange flavor gelatin with fresh peaches; lime flavor with melon balls; or strawberry flavor with strawberries, bananas and/or blueberries.

  1 cup fresh fruit
  ¾ cup boiling water
  1 package (4-serving size) JELL-O Brand
      Sugar Free Low Calorie Gelatin Dessert or
      JELL-O Brand Gelatin Dessert, any flavor
  ½ cup cold water
      Ice cubes
  ¾ cup thawed COOL WHIP FREE or
      COOL WHIP LITE Whipped Topping

DIVIDE fruit among 6 parfait glasses.

STIR boiling water into gelatin in medium bowl at least 2 minutes until completely dissolved. Mix cold water and ice cubes to make 1¼ cups. Add to gelatin, stirring until slightly thickened. Remove any remaining ice. Measure ¾ cup of the gelatin; pour into parfait glasses. Refrigerate 1 hour or until set but not firm (gelatin should stick to finger when touched and should mound).

STIR whipped topping into remaining gelatin with wire whisk until smooth. Spoon over gelatin in glasses.

REFRIGERATE 1 hour or until firm. Garnish as desired. *Makes 6 servings*

Nutrition Information Per Serving (using ½ cup each blueberries and strawberries, JELL-O Brand Sugar Free Low Calorie Gelatin Dessert and COOL WHIP FREE and omitting cookies): 35 calories, 0.5g fat, 0mg cholesterol, 55mg sodium, 6g carbohydrate, less than 1g dietary fiber, 3g sugars, 1g protein, 15% daily value vitamin C

Preparation Time: 20 minutes
Refrigerating Time: 2 hours

Pudding in a Cloud

How to please the family in just 15 minutes.

2 cups thawed COOL WHIP Whipped Topping
2 cups cold milk
1 package (4-serving size) JELL-O Instant
Pudding & Pie Filling, any flavor

Amuse the kids by letting them make faces on the pudding with pieces of marshmallow, gumdrops or decorating gel.

SPOON whipped topping evenly into 6 dessert dishes. Using back of spoon, spread whipped topping onto bottom and up side of each dish.

POUR milk into medium bowl. Add pudding mix. Beat with wire whisk 2 minutes. Let stand 5 minutes. Spoon pudding into center of whipped topping.

REFRIGERATE until ready to serve.

Makes 6 servings

Preparation Time: 15 minutes
Refrigerating Time: 2 hours

JELL-O®
Fun Facts

In the early 1920's, Angus McDonall created a series of JELL-O illustrations under the banner of "America's Most Famous Dessert At Home Everywhere." These depictions showed JELL-O served by a monk in mission country, eyed by a bear in the mountains, placed on a prairie lunch table, eaten on a doorstop in New England, washed up on a desert island, and carried into an igloo under northern lights.

Dirt Cups

Great kid appeal here!

This recipe was developed in 1989 as part of the JELL-O Snacktivities® campaign to encourage parents and kids to make fun recipes together.

1 package (16 ounces) chocolate sandwich cookies
2 cups cold milk
1 package (4-serving size) JELL-O Chocolate Flavor Instant Pudding & Pie Filling
1 tub (8 ounces) COOL WHIP Whipped Topping, thawed
8 to 10 (7-ounce) paper or plastic cups
  Suggested garnishes: gummy worms or other gummy candies, candy flowers, chopped peanuts, granola

CRUSH cookies in zipper-style plastic bag with rolling pin or in food processor.

POUR milk into large bowl. Add pudding mix. Beat with wire whisk 2 minutes. Stir in whipped topping and ½ of the crushed cookies.

PLACE about 1 tablespoon of the crushed cookies in each cup. Fill cups about ¾ full with pudding mixture. Top with remaining crushed cookies.

REFRIGERATE until ready to serve. Garnish as desired.   *Makes 8 to 10 servings*

Sand Cups: Use 1 package (12 ounces) vanilla wafer cookies and JELL-O Vanilla Flavor Instant Pudding & Pie Filling.

Preparation Time: 15 minutes
Refrigerating Time: 2 hours

Left to right: Sand Cups, Dirt Cups

All-Time Favorites

Under-the-Sea Salad

Delightfully tangy with a hint of cinnamon.

> 1 can (16 ounces) pear halves in syrup, undrained
> 1 cup boiling water
> 1 package (4-serving size) JELL-O Brand Lime Flavor Gelatin Dessert
> ¼ teaspoon salt (optional)
> 1 tablespoon lemon juice
> 2 packages (3 ounces each) PHILADELPHIA BRAND Cream Cheese, softened
> ⅛ teaspoon ground cinnamon (optional)

DRAIN pears, reserving ¾ cup of the syrup. Dice pears; set aside.

STIR boiling water into gelatin and salt in medium bowl at least 2 minutes until completely dissolved. Stir in reserved syrup and lemon juice. Pour 1¼ cups gelatin into 4-cup mold or 8×4-inch loaf pan. Refrigerate about 1 hour or until set but not firm (gelatin should stick to finger when touched and should mound).

MEANWHILE, stir remaining gelatin gradually into cream cheese in large bowl with wire whisk until smooth. Stir in pears and cinnamon. Spoon over gelatin layer in mold.

REFRIGERATE 4 hours or until firm. Unmold. Garnish as desired.

Makes 6 servings

Preparation Time: 20 minutes
Refrigerating Time: 5 hours

Top to bottom: Vanilla Rice Pudding (page 45), Chocolate Swirl Cheesecake (page 48),
Under-the-Sea Salad, Ribbon Squares (page 44)

Crown Jewel Dessert

Shimmering gems of JELL-O make this mold extra special.

The concept of creamy gelatin with clear cubes originated in 1955 with a recipe called Broken Window Glass Cake.

1 package (4-serving size) JELL-O Brand Lime Flavor Gelatin Dessert*

1 package (4-serving size) JELL-O Brand Orange Flavor Gelatin Dessert*

1 package (4-serving size) JELL-O Brand Strawberry Flavor Gelatin Dessert*

3 cups boiling water

1½ cups cold water

1 cup boiling water

1 package (4-serving size) JELL-O Brand Strawberry Flavor Gelatin Dessert

½ cup cold water

1 tub (8 ounces) COOL WHIP Whipped Topping, thawed

PREPARE lime, orange and 1 package strawberry gelatin separately as directed on packages, using 1 cup boiling water and ½ cup cold water for each. Pour each flavor into separate 8-inch square pans. Refrigerate 4 hours or until firm. Cut into ½-inch cubes; measure 1½ cups of each flavor. (Use the remaining gelatin cubes for garnish if desired or for snacking.)

STIR 1 cup boiling water into remaining package of strawberry gelatin in medium bowl at least 2 minutes until completely dissolved. Stir in ½ cup cold water. Refrigerate 45 minutes or until slightly thickened (consistency of unbeaten egg whites).

STIR in ½ of the whipped topping. Gently stir in measured gelatin cubes. Pour into 9×5-inch loaf pan.

REFRIGERATE 4 hours or until firm. Unmold. Garnish with remaining whipped topping and gelatin cubes, if desired.   *Makes 16 servings*

*Or use any 3 different flavors of JELL-O Brand Gelatin Dessert.

Preparation Time: 45 minutes
Refrigerating Time: 8¾ hours

Crown Jewel Dessert

Ribbon Squares

3 cups boiling water
1 package (4-serving size) JELL-O Brand Gelatin Dessert, any red flavor
1 package (4-serving size) JELL-O Brand Lemon Flavor Gelatin Dessert
1 package (4-serving size) JELL-O Brand Lime Flavor Gelatin Dessert
1½ cups cold water
1 package (8 ounces) PHILADELPHIA BRAND Cream Cheese, softened
1 can (8 ounces) crushed pineapple in juice, undrained
1 cup thawed COOL WHIP Whipped Topping
½ cup KRAFT Mayo: Real Mayonnaise

STIR 1 cup boiling water into each flavor of gelatin in separate medium bowls at least 2 minutes until completely dissolved. Stir ¾ cup of the cold water into red gelatin. Pour into 9-inch square pan. Refrigerate about 45 minutes or until set but not firm (gelatin should stick to finger when touched and should mound).

MEANWHILE, stir lemon gelatin gradually into cream cheese in large bowl with wire whisk until smooth. Stir in pineapple with juice. Refrigerate about 45 minutes or until slightly thickened (consistency of unbeaten egg whites). Stir in whipped topping and mayonnaise. Spoon over red gelatin layer in pan. Refrigerate about 30 minutes or until set but not firm (gelatin should stick to finger when touched and should mound).

MEANWHILE, stir remaining ¾ cup cold water into lime gelatin. Refrigerate about 30 minutes or until slightly thickened (consistency of unbeaten egg whites). Spoon over lemon gelatin mixture in pan.

REFRIGERATE 4 hours or until firm. Unmold. Cut into squares. Garnish as desired.

Makes 9 servings

Preparation Time: 30 minutes
Refrigerating Time: 5¼ hours

Vanilla Rice Pudding

Comfort food at its best—quick and easy, too.

1 package (4-serving size) JELL-O Vanilla or Coconut Cream Flavor Cook & Serve Pudding & Pie Filling (*not Instant*)
4 cups milk
1 egg, well beaten
1 cup MINUTE Original Instant Enriched Rice, uncooked
¼ cup raisins (optional)
¼ teaspoon ground cinnamon*
⅛ teaspoon ground nutmeg*

Created in 1959 for a MINUTE Rice advertisement, Vanilla Rice Pudding combined two early convenience products to make a favorite traditional family dessert.

STIR pudding mix into milk and egg in large saucepan. Stir in rice and raisins.

STIRRING constantly, cook on medium heat until mixture comes to full boil. Remove from heat. Cool 5 minutes, stirring twice.

POUR into dessert dishes or serving bowl. Serve warm or refrigerate until ready to serve. (For chilled pudding, place plastic wrap on surface of hot pudding. Refrigerate about 1 hour. Stir before serving.) Sprinkle with cinnamon and nutmeg. Garnish as desired.   *Makes 8 servings*

*Cinnamon and nutmeg can be added before cooking but pudding will be darker.

Note: *Recipe can be doubled.*

Preparation Time: 5 minutes
Cooking Time: 25 minutes

Striped Delight

This perennial favorite, combining cream cheese, whipped topping and instant pudding, was first made in 1983 and was originally called Cream Cheese Pudding Dessert.

A potluck favorite, this creamy dessert features a chocolatey pudding layer over a pecan shortbread crust.

1 cup flour
1 cup finely chopped pecans
¼ cup sugar (optional)
½ cup (1 stick) butter or margarine, melted
1 package (8 ounces) PHILADELPHIA BRAND Cream Cheese, softened
¼ cup sugar
2 tablespoons milk
1 tub (8 ounces) COOL WHIP Whipped Topping, thawed
3½ cups cold milk
2 packages (4-serving size) JELL-O Chocolate Flavor Instant Pudding & Pie Filling

HEAT oven to 350°F.

MIX flour, pecans and ¼ cup sugar in 13×9-inch baking pan. Stir in butter until flour is moistened. Press firmly onto bottom of pan. Bake 20 minutes or until lightly browned. Cool.

BEAT cream cheese, ¼ cup sugar and 2 tablespoons milk in large bowl with wire whisk until smooth. Gently stir in ½ of the whipped topping. Spread onto cooled crust.

POUR 3½ cups milk into large bowl. Add pudding mixes. Beat with wire whisk 1 to 2 minutes or until well blended. Pour over cream cheese layer.

REFRIGERATE 4 hours or until set. Just before serving, spread remaining whipped topping over pudding. Garnish as desired.

Makes 15 servings

Preparation Time: 30 minutes
Baking Time: 20 minutes
Refrigerating Time: 4 hours

Striped Delight

Chocolate Swirl Cheesecake

Create this elegant showpiece dessert in just minutes.

> 1 package (11.1 ounces) JELL-O No
>   Bake Real Cheesecake
> 2 tablespoons sugar
> ⅓ cup butter or margarine, melted
> 2 squares BAKER'S Semi-Sweet
>   Baking Chocolate
> 1½ cups cold milk, divided

MIX crumbs, sugar and butter thoroughly with fork in 9-inch pie plate until crumbs are well moistened. Press firmly against side of pie plate first, using finger or large spoon to shape edge. Press remaining crumbs firmly onto bottom of pie plate using measuring cup.

MICROWAVE chocolate and 2 tablespoons of the milk in microwavable bowl on HIGH 1½ minutes or until chocolate is almost melted. Stir until chocolate is completely melted.

BEAT remaining milk and filling mix with electric mixer on low speed until blended. Beat on medium speed 3 minutes. (Filling will be thick.) Spoon 2 cups of the filling into crust. Stir chocolate mixture into remaining filling. Spoon over cheesecake. Swirl with knife to marbleize.

REFRIGERATE at least 1 hour.

Makes 8 servings

Preparation Time: 15 minutes
Refrigerating Time: 1 hour

"Never Do to be Without Jell-O."

As Tommy finished the Jell-O dessert at dinner mamma remarked, "That's the last of the Jell-O in the house," and he proceeded to the kitchen to enter an order for more.

"Never do to be without Jell-O," Tommy says.

Good idea, too, for with

JELL-O®

in the house you have something to rely on in time of emergency and all other times.

Any woman can make a dozen or more different kinds of dishes from each of the six flavors of Jell-O, which are: Strawberry, Raspberry, Orange, Lemon, Cherry, Chocolate.

Send for the 1920 Jell-O Book, which contains some new recipes for popular dishes.

THE GENESEE PURE FOOD COMPANY
Le Roy, N. Y., and Bridgeburg, Ont.

1921

Better-Than-S_x Cake

Try it . . . you'll like it!

1½ cups graham cracker crumbs

⅔ cup chopped pecans, divided

½ cup (1 stick) butter or margarine, melted

6 tablespoons sugar

1 package (8 ounces) PHILADELPHIA BRAND Cream Cheese, softened

3½ cups cold milk

2 packages (4-serving size) JELL-O Vanilla Flavor Instant Pudding & Pie Filling

1⅓ cups BAKER'S ANGEL FLAKE Coconut, divided

1 tub (8 ounces) COOL WHIP Whipped Topping, thawed

This rich layered pudding dessert, created in 1980 as Layered Coconut Pecan Delight, just shows how times change but good taste doesn't!

MIX crumbs, ⅓ cup of the pecans, butter and sugar in 13×9-inch pan. Press firmly onto bottom of pan.

BEAT cream cheese in large bowl with electric mixer on low speed until smooth. Gradually beat in ½ cup of the milk. Add remaining milk and the pudding mixes. Beat on low speed about 2 minutes or until well blended. Stir in 1 cup of the coconut. Pour immediately over crust. Spread whipped topping evenly over the pudding mixture.

REFRIGERATE 2 hours or until set. Toast remaining ⅓ cup coconut and ⅓ cup pecans. Sprinkle over top of dessert.   *Makes 15 servings*

Preparation Time: 30 minutes
Refrigerating Time: 2 hours

Rainbow Ribbon Mold

A real showpiece for a buffet or dinner party.

Gelatin recipes with layers of different flavors and textures date back to the early 1900's when they were called Neapolitans. They were often molded in loaf pans and served in slices to show the rainbow effect.

6¼ cups boiling water
5 packages (4-serving size) JELL-O Brand
Gelatin Dessert, any 5 different flavors
1 cup (½ pint) BREAKSTONE'S Sour Cream
or BREYERS Vanilla Lowfat Yogurt

STIR 1¼ cups boiling water into 1 flavor of gelatin in small bowl at least 2 minutes until completely dissolved. Pour ¾ cup of the dissolved gelatin into 6-cup ring mold. Refrigerate about 15 minutes until set but not firm (gelatin should stick to finger when touched and should mound). Refrigerate remaining gelatin in bowl about 5 minutes until slightly thickened (consistency of unbeaten egg whites). Gradually stir in 3 tablespoons of the sour cream. Spoon over gelatin in pan. Refrigerate about 15 minutes or until set but not firm (gelatin should stick to finger when touched and should mound).

MEANWHILE, repeat process with each remaining gelatin flavor. (Be sure to cool dissolved gelatin to room temperature before pouring into mold.) Refrigerate gelatin as directed to create a total of 10 alternating clear and creamy gelatin layers.

REFRIGERATE 2 hours or until firm. Unmold. Garnish as desired. *Makes 12 servings*

Preparation Time: 1 hour
Refrigerating Time: 4½ hours

JELL-O
Fun Facts

JELL-O gelatin is the largest-selling prepared dessert in America.

Rainbow Ribbon Mold

Creamy Vanilla Sauce

An elegant topping for fresh fruit or gingerbread.

Developed in 1981 for a JELL-O Instant Pudding advertisement, variations on this sauce made with other pudding flavors have topped many a dessert.

3½ cups cold milk, light cream or half-and-half
1 package (4-serving size) JELL-O Vanilla or French Vanilla Flavor Instant Pudding & Pie Filling

POUR milk into bowl. Add pudding mix. Beat with wire whisk 2 minutes. Cover.

REFRIGERATE until ready to serve. Serve over your favorite fruits or cake. Garnish as desired.

Makes 3½ cups

Creamy Citrus Sauce: Add 2 teaspoons grated orange peel with pudding mix.

Preparation Time: 5 minutes

Watergate Salad (Pistachio Pineapple Delight)

Serve as a salad with cold sliced cooked chicken or as dessert on its own.

Originally named Pistachio Pineapple Delight, Watergate Salad first surfaced in 1976, the year Pistachio Flavor Instant Pudding & Pie Filling was launched.

1 package (4-serving size) JELL-O Pistachio Flavor Instant Pudding & Pie Filling
1 can (20 ounces) crushed pineapple in juice, undrained
1 cup miniature marshmallows
½ cup chopped nuts
2 cups thawed COOL WHIP Whipped Topping

STIR pudding mix, pineapple with juice, marshmallows and nuts in large bowl until well blended. Gently stir in whipped topping.

REFRIGERATE 1 hour or until ready to serve. Garnish as desired.

Makes 8 servings

Preparation Time: 10 minutes
Refrigerating Time: 1 hour

Dream Pie

This heavenly pie lives up to its name.

> 2 envelopes **DREAM WHIP Whipped Topping Mix**
> 2¾ **cups cold milk, divided**
> 1 **teaspoon vanilla**
> 2 **packages (4-serving size) JELL-O Instant Pudding & Pie Filling, any flavor**
> 1 **baked pastry shell (9 inch), cooled, or**
> 1 **prepared graham cracker or chocolate flavor crumb crust (6 ounces)**

During World War II, one-crust pies became popular because of the scarcity of shortening. Many were filled with JELL-O gelatin or pudding—convenient products for women involved in the war effort.

BEAT whipped topping mix, 1 cup of the milk and vanilla in large bowl with electric mixer on high speed 6 minutes or until topping thickens and forms peaks.

ADD remaining 1¾ cups milk and pudding mixes; beat on low speed until blended. Beat on high speed 2 minutes, scraping bowl occasionally. Spoon into pastry shell.

REFRIGERATE at least 4 hours.

Makes 8 servings

Preparation Time: 15 minutes
Refrigerating Time: 4 hours

JELL-O Fun Facts

In 1913, Rosie O'Neill, creator of the famous rosy-cheeked Kewpie Dolls, illustrated a full-color Kewpie Doll JELL-O Book, showing the little imps making and garnishing a variety of beautiful salads and desserts.

Luscious Pies

Strawberry Lime Pie

This fluffy concoction beautifully complements the tartness of fresh berries.

- ⅔ **cup boiling water**
- 1 **package (4-serving size) JELL-O Brand Lime Flavor Gelatin Dessert**
- ½ **teaspoon grated lime peel**
- 2 **tablespoons lime juice**
- ½ **cup cold water**
  Ice cubes
- 1 **tub (8 ounces) COOL WHIP Whipped Topping, thawed**
- 1 **cup sliced strawberries**
- 1 **prepared graham cracker crumb crust (6 ounces)**

STIR boiling water into gelatin in large bowl at least 2 minutes until completely dissolved. Stir in lime peel and juice. Mix cold water and ice to make 1 cup. Add to gelatin, stirring until slightly thickened. Remove any remaining ice.

STIR in 2½ cups of the whipped topping with wire whisk until smooth. Gently stir in strawberries. Refrigerate 30 minutes or until mixture is very thick and will mound. Spoon into crust.

REFRIGERATE 4 hours or until firm. Top with remaining whipped topping. Garnish as desired.   *Makes 8 servings*

Preparation Time: 20 minutes
Refrigerating Time: 4½ hours

Top to bottom: Glazed Fruit Pie (page 58), Cookies-and-Cream Ice Cream Shop Pie (page 59), Strawberry Lime Pie, White Chocolate-Devil's Food Pie (page 66)

COOL 'N EASY® Pie

Ten minutes in the morning—luscious strawberry pie in the evening!

⅔ cup boiling water
1 package (4-serving size) JELL-O Brand Gelatin Dessert, any red flavor
½ cup cold water
  Ice cubes
1 tub (8 ounces) COOL WHIP Whipped Topping, thawed
1 cup chopped strawberries
1 prepared graham cracker crumb crust (6 ounces)

STIR boiling water into gelatin in large bowl at least 2 minutes until completely dissolved. Mix cold water and ice to make 1¼ cups. Add to gelatin, stirring until slightly thickened. Remove any remaining ice.

STIR in whipped topping with wire whisk until smooth. Mix in strawberries. Refrigerate 20 to 30 minutes or until mixture is very thick and will mound. Spoon into crust.

REFRIGERATE 6 hours or overnight until firm. Garnish as desired.

Makes 8 servings

Preparation Time: 10 minutes
Refrigerating Time: 6½ hours

America's most famous dessert

JELL-O

1925

57

COOL 'N EASY® Pie

Glazed Fruit Pie

This creamy pie, topped with fruit encased in clear gelatin, was first featured in a 1985 television commercial for JELL-O brand pudding.

Try different fruits and JELL-O pudding flavors to create variations of this fabulous pie.

- 1½ cups cold milk or half-and-half
- 1 package (4-serving size) JELL-O Vanilla Flavor Instant Pudding & Pie Filling
- 1 prepared graham cracker crumb crust (6 ounces) or 1 baked pastry shell (9 inch), cooled
- 1 cup boiling water
- 1 package (4-serving size) JELL-O Brand Lemon, Peach or Orange Flavor Gelatin Dessert, or any red flavor
- ½ cup cold water
- 1½ cups fresh or drained canned fruit*

POUR milk into large bowl. Add pudding mix. Beat with wire whisk 1 minute. Pour into crust. Refrigerate 1 hour.

STIR boiling water into gelatin in large bowl at least 2 minutes until completely dissolved. Stir in cold water. Refrigerate 1 hour or until thickened (spoon drawn through leaves definite impression). Pour 1 cup gelatin over the pudding layer. Arrange fruit on gelatin. Spoon remaining gelatin over fruit.

REFRIGERATE 2 hours or until firm.

Makes 8 servings

*Use any variety of berries, mandarin orange sections, sliced bananas, peaches or plums, or halved seedless grapes.

Preparation Time: 15 minutes
Refrigerating Time: 4 hours

Ice Cream Shop Pie

Favorite ice cream flavors in a quick-to-make pie.

1½ cups cold milk, half-and-half or light cream
1 package (4-serving size) JELL-O Instant
   Pudding & Pie Filling
1 tub (8 ounces) COOL WHIP Whipped
   Topping, thawed
1 prepared crumb crust (6 ounces)

Instant pudding & pie filling and whipped topping provide the base for these delectable freezer pies with a variety of stir-in ingredients.

POUR milk into large bowl. Add pudding mix. Beat with wire whisk 2 minutes. Gently stir in whipped topping. Spoon into crust.

FREEZE 6 hours or overnight until firm. Let stand at room temperature or in refrigerator 15 minutes or until pie can be cut easily.

GARNISH as desired.   *Makes 8 servings*

Cookies-and-Cream Pie: Use JELL-O Vanilla Flavor Instant Pudding & Pie Filling and chocolate crumb crust. Stir in 1 cup chopped chocolate sandwich cookies with whipped topping.

Rocky Road Pie: Use JELL-O Chocolate Flavor Instant Pudding & Pie Filling and chocolate crumb crust. Stir in ⅓ cup each BAKER'S Semi-Sweet Real Chocolate Chips, miniature marshmallows and chopped nuts with whipped topping. Serve with chocolate sauce, if desired.

Peanut Butter Pie: Use JELL-O Vanilla Flavor Instant Pudding & Pie Filling and graham cracker crumb crust. Reduce milk to 1 cup and add ½ cup peanut butter with pudding mix. Serve with chocolate sauce and chopped peanuts, if desired.

Preparation Time: 15 minutes
Freezing Time: 6 hours

Lemon Chiffon Pie

Cool, easy and incredibly delicious!

No need to separate eggs and beat the whites for this airy pie. Just follow these simple preparation steps.

⅔ cup boiling water
1 package (4-serving size) JELL-O Brand
    Lemon Flavor Gelatin Dessert
2 teaspoons grated lemon peel
2 tablespoons lemon juice
½ cup cold water
    Ice cubes
1 tub (8 ounces) COOL WHIP Whipped
    Topping, thawed
1 prepared graham cracker crumb crust
    (6 ounces)

STIR boiling water into gelatin in large bowl at least 2 minutes until completely dissolved. Stir in lemon peel and juice. Mix cold water and ice to make 1¼ cups. Add to gelatin, stirring until slightly thickened. Remove any remaining ice.

STIR in whipped topping with wire whisk until smooth. Refrigerate 20 to 30 minutes or until mixture is very thick and will mound. Spoon into crust.

REFRIGERATE 6 hours or overnight until firm. Garnish as desired.   *Makes 8 servings*

Preparation Time: 20 minutes
Refrigerating Time: 6½ hours

Lemon Chiffon Pie

Double Layer Chocolate Pie

To quickly soften cream cheese, microwave on HIGH for 15 to 20 seconds.

4 ounces PHILADELPHIA BRAND Cream Cheese, softened
1 tablespoon milk or half-and-half
1 tablespoon sugar
1 tub (8 ounces) COOL WHIP Whipped Topping, thawed
1 prepared chocolate flavor crumb crust (6 ounces)
2 cups cold milk or half-and-half
2 packages (4-serving size) JELL-O Chocolate Flavor Instant Pudding & Pie Filling

MIX cream cheese, 1 tablespoon milk and sugar in large bowl with wire whisk until smooth. Gently stir in 1½ cups of the whipped topping. Spread onto bottom of crust.

POUR 2 cups milk into bowl. Add pudding mixes. Beat with wire whisk until well mixed. (Mixture will be thick.) Immediately stir in remaining whipped topping. Spread over cream cheese layer.

REFRIGERATE 4 hours or until set. Garnish as desired.   *Makes 8 servings*

Preparation Time: 15 minutes
Refrigerating Time: 4 hours

JELL-O Fun Facts

In addition to Bill Cosby, famous spokespeople for JELL-O have included Jack Benny, Andy Griffith and Ethel Barrymore.

Double Layer Chocolate Pie

Summer Berry Pie

Pure joy is this fresh berry pie!

Strawberry is, hands down, the most popular flavor of JELL-O and has been for 100 years.

¾ cup sugar
3 tablespoons cornstarch
1½ cups water
1 package (4-serving size) JELL-O Brand Gelatin Dessert, any red flavor
1 cup blueberries
1 cup raspberries
1 cup sliced strawberries
1 prepared graham cracker crumb crust (6 ounces)
2 cups thawed COOL WHIP Whipped Topping

MIX sugar and cornstarch in medium saucepan. Gradually stir in water until smooth. Stirring constantly, cook on medium heat until mixture comes to boil; boil 1 minute. Remove from heat. Stir in gelatin until completely dissolved. Cool to room temperature. Stir in berries. Pour into crust.

REFRIGERATE 3 hours or until firm. Top with whipped topping.   *Makes 8 servings*

Preparation Time: 20 minutes
Refrigerating Time: 3 hours

JELL-O *Fun Facts*

Every day more than 820,000 packages of JELL-O are purchased or prepared and eaten.

Summer Berry Pie

White Chocolate-Devil's Food Pie

JELL-O Fat Free Instant Pudding & Pie Filling, specially formulated to work with skim milk, was introduced in 1994 for those seeking ways to reduce fat in their diets.

Creamy dark and white chocolate pudding layers team together to make a scrumptious dessert.

> 2 cups cold skim milk, divided
> 1 package (4-serving size) JELL-O Devil's Food Flavor Fat Free Instant Pudding & Pie Filling
> 1 tub (8 ounces) COOL WHIP FREE or COOL WHIP LITE Whipped Topping, thawed
> 1 prepared reduced fat graham cracker crumb crust (6 ounces)
> 1 package (4-serving size) JELL-O White Chocolate Flavor Fat Free Instant Pudding & Pie Filling

POUR 1 cup of the milk into medium bowl. Add devil's food flavor pudding mix. Beat with wire whisk 1 minute. (Mixture will be thick.) Gently stir in ½ of the whipped topping. Spoon evenly into crust.

POUR remaining 1 cup milk into another medium bowl. Add white chocolate flavor pudding mix. Beat with wire whisk 1 minute. (Mixture will be thick.) Gently stir in remaining whipped topping. Spread over pudding layer in crust.

REFRIGERATE 4 hours or until set. Garnish as desired.   *Makes 8 servings*

Nutrition Information Per Serving (using COOL WHIP FREE and omitting garnish): 270 calories, 5g fat, 0mg cholesterol, 490mg sodium, 53g carbohydrate, less than 1g dietary fiber, 4g protein, 10% daily value calcium

Preparation Time: 10 minutes
Refrigerating Time: 4 hours

Creamy Chocolate Pie

This will delight family and guests alike.

1¾ **cups cold milk**
  2 **packages (4-serving size) JELL-O Chocolate**
      or Chocolate Fudge Flavor Instant
      Pudding & Pie Filling
  1 **tub (8 ounces) COOL WHIP Whipped**
      Topping, thawed
  1 **prepared chocolate flavor crumb crust**
      (6 ounces)

Preparation time for this luscious pie takes only 10 minutes.

POUR milk into large bowl. Add pudding mixes. Beat with wire whisk until well mixed. (Mixture will be thick.) Immediately stir in whipped topping. Spoon into crust.

REFRIGERATE 4 hours or until set. Garnish as desired. *Makes 8 servings*

Preparation Time: 10 minutes
Refrigerating Time: 4 hours

JELL-O Fun Facts

A JELL-O cartoon ad contest in 1921 challenged people to write or design a JELL-O ad. The $200 first prize was awarded based on "intelligence, composition, neatness, originality and availability." The winning ad and a photo of the creator were published four months later. The prize money was used to buy a horse.

Sensational Desserts

Pudding Poke Cake

A favorite with everyone . . . and so easy to make.

1 package (2-layer size) chocolate cake mix or cake mix with pudding in the mix

4 cups cold milk

2 packages (4-serving size) JELL-O Vanilla Flavor Instant Pudding & Pie Filling

PREPARE and bake cake mix as directed on package for 13×9-inch baking pan. Remove from oven. Immediately poke holes down through cake to pan at 1-inch intervals with round handle of a wooden spoon. (Or poke holes with a plastic drinking straw, using turning motion to make large holes.)

POUR milk into large bowl. Add pudding mixes. Beat with wire whisk 2 minutes. Quickly pour about ½ of the thin pudding mixture evenly over warm cake and into holes. Let remaining pudding mixture stand to thicken slightly. Spoon over top of cake, swirling to frost cake.

REFRIGERATE at least 1 hour or until ready to serve.

Makes 15 servings

Preparation Time: 30 minutes
Baking Time: 40 minutes
Refrigerating Time: 1 hour

Top to bottom: Strawberry Lime Dessert (page 73), Orange Pineapple Layered Dessert (page 72), Layered Chocolate Cheesecake Squares (page 77), Pudding Poke Cake

White Chocolate Cheesecake

A truly luxurious dessert with a rich, silky texture.

> 1 package (11.1 ounces) JELL-O No Bake Real Cheesecake
> 2 tablespoons sugar
> ⅓ cup butter or margarine, melted
> 1½ cups cold milk
> 1 package (6 squares) BAKER'S Premium White Baking Chocolate Squares, melted
> 2 squares BAKER'S Semi-Sweet Baking Chocolate, melted (optional)

MIX crumbs, sugar and butter thoroughly with fork in 9-inch pie plate until crumbs are well moistened. Press firmly against side of pie plate first, using finger or large spoon to shape edge. Press remaining crumbs firmly onto bottom of pie plate using measuring cup.

BEAT milk and filling mix with electric mixer on low speed until blended. Beat on medium speed 3 minutes. (Filling will be thick.) Reserve about 3 tablespoons melted white chocolate for garnish, if desired. Stir remaining melted white chocolate into filling mixture. Spoon into crust. Drizzle with reserved melted white chocolate and melted semi-sweet chocolate, if desired.

REFRIGERATE at least 1 hour, if desired.

Makes 8 servings

Preparation Time: 15 minutes
Refrigerating Time: 1 hour

1946

White Chocolate Cheesecake

Orange Pineapple Layered Dessert

Some fruits sink and others float when added to JELL-O. Sinkers include mandarin oranges, seedless grapes and drained slices or chunks of canned fruits. Floaters are slices of banana, apple, strawberries, fresh peaches and pears, and fresh orange sections.

Even the kids will love this tasty dessert perfect for family gatherings.

1½ **cups boiling water**
1 **package (8-serving size) or 2 packages (4-serving size) JELL-O Brand Orange Flavor Gelatin Dessert**
1 **cup cold water**
1 **can (20 ounces) crushed pineapple in juice, undrained**
1 **can (11 ounces) mandarin orange segments, drained**
1½ **cups graham cracker crumbs**
½ **cup sugar, divided**
½ **cup (1 stick) butter or margarine, melted**
1 **package (8 ounces) PHILADELPHIA BRAND Cream Cheese, softened**
2 **tablespoons milk**
1 **tub (8 ounces) COOL WHIP Whipped Topping, thawed**

STIR boiling water into gelatin in large bowl at least 2 minutes until completely dissolved. Stir in cold water, pineapple with juice and oranges. Refrigerate about 1¼ hours or until slightly thickened (consistency of unbeaten egg whites).

MIX crumbs, ¼ cup of the sugar and butter in 13×9-inch pan. Press firmly onto bottom of pan. Refrigerate until ready to fill.

BEAT cream cheese, remaining ¼ cup sugar and milk in large bowl until smooth. Gently stir in 2 cups of the whipped topping. Spread evenly over crust. Spoon gelatin over cream cheese layer.

REFRIGERATE 3 hours or until firm. Garnish with remaining whipped topping.   *Makes 15 servings*

Preparation Time: 30 minutes
Refrigerating Time: 4¼ hours

Strawberry Lime Dessert

2 cups boiling water
1 package (4-serving size) JELL-O Brand Lime Flavor Sugar Free Low Calorie Gelatin Dessert or JELL-O Brand Lime Flavor Gelatin Dessert
½ cup cold water
1 container (8 ounces) BREYERS Vanilla Lowfat Yogurt
1 package (4-serving size) JELL-O Brand Strawberry Flavor Sugar Free Low Calorie Gelatin Dessert or JELL-O Brand Strawberry Flavor Gelatin Dessert
1 package (10 ounces) frozen strawberries in lite syrup, unthawed

Fruits frequently used in early recipes were strawberries, peaches, pineapple, apricots, cherries, prunes, raisins, dates and bananas.

STIR 1 cup of the boiling water into lime gelatin in medium bowl at least 2 minutes until completely dissolved. Stir in cold water. Refrigerate about 45 minutes or until slightly thickened (consistency of unbeaten egg whites). Stir in yogurt with wire whisk until smooth. Pour into 2-quart serving bowl. Refrigerate about 15 minutes or until set but not firm (gelatin should stick to finger when touched and should mound).

STIR remaining 1 cup boiling water into strawberry gelatin in medium bowl at least 2 minutes until completely dissolved. Stir in frozen berries until berries are separated and gelatin is thickened (spoon drawn through leaves definite impression). Spoon over lime gelatin mixture.

REFRIGERATE 2 hours or until firm. Garnish as desired.   *Makes 10 servings*

Nutrition Information Per Serving (using JELL-O Brand Strawberry and Lime Flavors Sugar Free Low Calorie Gelatin Dessert and omitting garnish): 60 calories, 0g fat, less than 5mg cholesterol, 65mg sodium, 11g carbohydrate, less than 1g dietary fiber, 9g sugars, 2g protein, 15% daily value vitamin C

Preparation Time: 15 minutes
Refrigerating Time: 3 hours

Peach Melba Dessert

Peach Melba was created in the late 1800's by renowned French chef Escoffier for Dame Nellie Melba, an Australian opera singer. The original version featured peach halves topped with vanilla ice cream, raspberry sauce, whipped cream and sliced almonds.

1½ **cups boiling water**
2 **packages (4-serving size) JELL-O Brand Raspberry Flavor Sugar Free Low Calorie Gelatin Dessert or JELL-O Brand Raspberry Flavor Gelatin Dessert**
1 **container (8 ounces) BREYERS Vanilla Lowfat Yogurt**
1 **cup raspberries, divided**
1 **can (8 ounces) peach slices in juice, undrained**
Cold water

STIR ¾ cup of the boiling water into 1 package of gelatin in large bowl at least 2 minutes until completely dissolved. Refrigerate about 1 hour or until slightly thickened (consistency of unbeaten egg whites). Stir in yogurt and ½ cup of the raspberries. Reserve remaining raspberries for garnish. Pour gelatin mixture into serving bowl. Refrigerate about 2 hours or until set but not firm (gelatin should stick to finger when touched and should mound).

MEANWHILE, drain peaches, reserving juice. Add cold water to reserved juice to make 1 cup; set aside. Stir remaining ¾ cup boiling water into remaining package of gelatin in large bowl at least 2 minutes until completely dissolved. Stir in measured juice and water. Refrigerate about 1 hour or until slightly thickened (consistency of unbeaten egg whites).

RESERVE several peach slices for garnish; chop remaining peaches. Stir chopped peaches into slightly thickened gelatin. Spoon over gelatin layer in bowl. Refrigerate 3 hours or until firm. Top with reserved fruits. *Makes 8 servings*

Nutrition Information Per Serving (using JELL-O Brand Raspberry Flavor Sugar Free Low Calorie Gelatin Dessert): 60 calories, 0g fat, less than 5mg cholesterol, 75mg sodium, 10g carbohydrate, 1g dietary fiber, 11g sugars, 3g protein

Preparation Time: 20 minutes
Refrigerating Time: 6 hours

Peach Melba Dessert

Fruity Pound Cake

A wonderfully moist cake with just the right touch of lemon.

> 1 package (4-serving size) JELL-O Brand Lemon Flavor Gelatin Dessert
> 1 teaspoon grated lemon or orange peel
> 1 package (2-layer size) white cake mix or cake mix with pudding in the mix
> ¾ cup water
> ¼ cup oil
> 4 eggs
> Fluffy Pudding Frosting (recipe follows)

ADD gelatin and grated peel to cake mix.

PREPARE and bake cake mix as directed on package in two 8- or 9-inch round cake pans. Cool 15 minutes; remove from pans. Cool completely on wire racks. Fill and frost with Fluffy Pudding Frosting. Decorate as desired.   *Makes 12 servings*

Fluffy Pudding Frosting: Pour 1 cup cold milk into medium bowl. Add 1 package (4-serving size) JELL-O Instant Pudding & Pie Filling, any flavor, and ¼ cup powdered sugar. Beat with wire whisk 2 minutes. Gently stir in 1 tub (8 ounces) COOL WHIP Whipped Topping, thawed. Spread onto cake at once. Makes about 4 cups or enough for two 8- or 9-inch layers.

Preparation Time: 30 minutes
Baking Time: 40 minutes

Layered Chocolate Cheesecake Squares

This is the ultimate dessert for dinner guests.

> 1 package (9.2 ounces) JELL-O No Bake Chocolate Silk Pie
> 1 package (11.1 ounces) JELL-O No Bake Real Cheesecake
> ½ cup (1 stick) butter or margarine, melted
> 1⅔ cups cold milk
> 1½ cups cold milk

This recipe was developed in 1984 with the introduction of JELL-O No Bake Chocolate Silk Pie.

MIX crumbs from both packages and butter thoroughly with fork in medium bowl until crumbs are well moistened. Press firmly onto bottom of foil-lined 13×9-inch pan.

PREPARE Chocolate Silk Pie and Cheesecake fillings, separately, as directed on each package. Spread chocolate filling evenly over crust; top with cheesecake filling.

REFRIGERATE at least 1 hour. Garnish as desired.

Makes 15 servings

Preparation Time: 20 minutes
Refrigerating Time: 1 hour

JELL-O Fun Facts

In 1943, a JELL-O ad featured singer Kate Smith with a wartime message on managing scarce and rationed foods: "We can be careful to buy and cook only what we need! And we can think up smart ways to use leftovers."

Berried Delight

A new berry season sensation.

In 1944, the JELL-O brand published a war-wise recipe booklet, "Bright Spots for Wartime Meals— 66 Ration-Wise Recipes," with tips for managing those precious ration points while adding a little eating pleasure at the same time.

1½ cups graham cracker crumbs
½ cup sugar, divided
½ cup (1 stick) butter or margarine, melted
1 package (8 ounces) PHILADELPHIA BRAND Cream Cheese, softened
2 tablespoons milk
1 tub (8 ounces) COOL WHIP Whipped Topping, thawed
2 pints strawberries, hulled, halved
3½ cups cold milk
2 packages (4-serving size) JELL-O Vanilla Flavor Instant Pudding & Pie Filling

MIX crumbs, ¼ cup of the sugar and butter in 13×9-inch pan. Press firmly onto bottom of pan. Refrigerate until ready to fill.

BEAT cream cheese, remaining ¼ cup sugar and 2 tablespoons milk until smooth. Gently stir in ½ of the whipped topping. Spread over crust. Top with strawberry halves.

POUR 3½ cups milk into large bowl. Add pudding mixes. Beat with wire whisk 2 minutes. Pour over cream cheese layer.

REFRIGERATE 4 hours or until set. Just before serving, spread remaining whipped topping over pudding.　　　　*Makes 15 servings*

Preparation Time: 30 minutes
Refrigerating Time: 4 hours

Berried Delight

Holiday Specialties

Holiday Poke Cake

This all-time favorite is appropriately red and green for the Yuletide festivities.

> 2 baked 8- or 9-inch round white cake layers, cooled completely
> 2 cups boiling water
> 1 package (4-serving size) JELL-O Brand Gelatin Dessert, any red flavor
> 1 package (4-serving size) JELL-O Brand Lime Flavor Gelatin Dessert
> 1 tub (8 or 12 ounces) COOL WHIP Whipped Topping, thawed

PLACE cake layers, top sides up, in 2 clean 8- or 9-inch round cake pans. Pierce cake with large fork at ½-inch intervals.

STIR 1 cup of the boiling water into each flavor of gelatin in separate bowls at least 2 minutes until completely dissolved. Carefully pour red gelatin over 1 cake layer and lime gelatin over second cake layer. Refrigerate 3 hours.

DIP 1 cake pan in warm water 10 seconds; unmold onto serving plate. Spread with about 1 cup of the whipped topping. Unmold second cake layer; carefully place on first cake layer. Frost top and side of cake with remaining whipped topping.

REFRIGERATE at least 1 hour or until ready to serve. Decorate as desired. *Makes 12 servings*

Preparation Time: 30 minutes
Refrigerating Time: 4 hours

*Top to bottom: Spiced Cranberry Orange Mold (page 86), Layered Cranberry Cheesecake (page 90),
Holiday Poke Cake, Praline Pumpkin Pie (page 87)*

Cranberry Fruit Mold

Experience delicious fruit-filled effervescence in this delightful mold!

2 cups boiling water

1 package (8-serving size) or
    2 packages (4-serving size) JELL-O Brand Cranberry Flavor Gelatin Dessert or JELL-O Brand Cranberry Flavor Sugar Free Low Calorie Gelatin Dessert

1½ cups cold ginger ale, lemon-lime carbonated beverage, seltzer or water

2 cups halved green and/or red seedless grapes

1 can (11 ounces) mandarin orange segments, drained

STIR boiling water into gelatin in large bowl at least 2 minutes until completely dissolved. Stir in cold ginger ale. Refrigerate about 1½ hours or until thickened (spoon drawn through leaves definite impression). Stir in fruit. Spoon into 6-cup mold.

REFRIGERATE 4 hours or until firm. Unmold. Garnish as desired.

Makes 10 servings

 ***Nutrition Information Per Serving (using JELL-O Brand Cranberry Flavor Sugar Free Low Calorie Gelatin Dessert and seltzer and omitting garnish):*** *45 calories, 0g fat, 0mg cholesterol, 65mg sodium, 10g carbohydrate, less than 1g dietary fiber, 8g sugars, 2g protein, 20% daily vitamin C*

Preparation Time: 15 minutes
Refrigerating Time: 5½ hours

June 23, 1956

Three little kittens took off their mittens
Enchanted, delighted and merry.
For each was to savor a new Jell-O flavor —
Black Raspberry, Grape and Black Cherry.

JELL-O
New!
IMITATION
BLACK CHERRY FLAVOR

1956

Cranberry Fruit Mold

Merry Cherry Holiday Dessert

An easy yet spectacular finale to any holiday meal.

Speed-scratch cooking has really taken hold in the 1990's. This recipe is a fine example of achieving great results with convenience products. After all, JELL-O was one of the first convenience products available.

1½ cups boiling water
  1 package (8-serving size) or 2 packages (4-serving size) JELL-O Brand Cherry Flavor Gelatin Dessert, or any red flavor
1½ cups cold water
  1 can (21 ounces) cherry pie filling
  4 cups angel food cake cubes
  3 cups cold milk
  2 packages (4-serving size) JELL-O Vanilla Flavor Instant Pudding & Pie Filling
  1 tub (8 ounces) COOL WHIP Whipped Topping, thawed

STIR boiling water into gelatin in large bowl at least 2 minutes until completely dissolved. Stir in cold water and cherry pie filling. Refrigerate about 1 hour or until slightly thickened (consistency of unbeaten egg whites). Place cake cubes in 3-quart serving bowl. Spoon gelatin mixture over cake. Refrigerate about 45 minutes or until set but not firm (gelatin should stick to finger when touched and should mound).

POUR milk into large bowl. Add pudding mixes. Beat with wire whisk 1 minute. Gently stir in 2 cups of the whipped topping. Spoon over gelatin mixture in bowl.

REFRIGERATE 2 hours or until set. Top with remaining whipped topping and garnish as desired.

Makes 16 servings

Preparation Time: 20 minutes
Refrigerating Time: 3¾ hours

Merry Cherry Holiday Dessert

Spiced Cranberry Orange Mold

Since its earliest days, JELL-O gelatin has been used as a "table jelly" to accompany meat and poultry. It is still prized for its delicious flavor and "delightful cooling quality."

No holiday dinner should be without this!

1½ cups boiling water
1 package (8-serving size) or 2 packages (4-serving size) JELL-O Brand Cranberry Flavor Gelatin, or any red flavor
1 can (16 ounces) whole berry cranberry sauce
1 cup cold water
1 tablespoon lemon juice
¼ teaspoon ground cinnamon
⅛ teaspoon ground cloves
1 orange, sectioned, diced
½ cup chopped walnuts

STIR boiling water into gelatin in large bowl at least 2 minutes until completely dissolved. Stir in cranberry sauce, cold water, lemon juice, cinnamon and cloves. Refrigerate about 1½ hours or until thickened (spoon drawn through leaves definite impression).

STIR in orange and walnuts. Spoon into 5-cup mold.

REFRIGERATE 4 hours or until firm. Unmold. Garnish as desired.   *Makes 10 servings*

Preparation Time: 20 minutes
Refrigerating Time: 5½ hours

Praline Pumpkin Pie

The praline layer adds fabulous taste and texture to this Thanksgiving pie.

- ½ **cup chopped pecans or walnuts**
- ⅓ **cup butter or margarine**
- ⅓ **cup firmly packed brown sugar**
- 1 **prepared graham cracker crumb crust (6 ounces)**
- 1 **cup cold milk**
- 1 **can (16 ounces) pumpkin**
- 2 **packages (4-serving size) JELL-O Vanilla Flavor Instant Pudding & Pie Filling**
- 1¼ **teaspoons pumpkin pie spice**
- 1½ **cups thawed COOL WHIP Whipped Topping**

Traditional pumpkin pies bake for nearly an hour. This one takes only about 20 minutes to prepare and requires no baking at all!

BRING nuts, butter and sugar to boil in small saucepan on medium heat; boil 30 seconds. Spread onto bottom of crust. Cool.

POUR milk into large bowl. Add pumpkin, pudding mixes and spice. Beat with wire whisk until well mixed. (Mixture will be thick.) Immediately stir in whipped topping. Spread over nut layer.

REFRIGERATE 4 hours or until set. Garnish as desired. *Makes 8 servings*

Preparation Time: 20 minutes
Refrigerating Time: 4 hours

JELL-O Fun Facts

Screen star Roy Rogers was the spokesman for JELL-O pudding in 1956.

Double Layer Pumpkin Pie

A noble ending to the Thanksgiving feast.

JELL-O pudding pumpkin pies date back to the 1960's. This 1991 recipe, featuring a scrumptious double layer, requires no baking whatsoever.

4 ounces PHILADELPHIA BRAND Cream Cheese, softened
1 tablespoon milk or half-and-half
1 tablespoon sugar
1½ cups thawed COOL WHIP Whipped Topping
1 prepared graham cracker crumb crust (6 ounces)
1 cup cold milk or half-and-half
1 can (16 ounces) pumpkin
2 packages (4-serving size) JELL-O Vanilla Flavor Instant Pudding & Pie Filling
1 teaspoon ground cinnamon
½ teaspoon ground ginger
¼ teaspoon ground cloves

MIX cream cheese, 1 tablespoon milk and sugar in large bowl with wire whisk until smooth. Gently stir in whipped topping. Spread onto bottom of crust.

POUR 1 cup milk into large bowl. Add pumpkin, pudding mixes and spices. Beat with wire whisk until well mixed. (Mixture will be thick.) Spread over cream cheese layer.

REFRIGERATE 4 hours or until set.

Makes 8 servings

Double Layer Pecan Pumpkin Pie: Stir ¼ cup toasted chopped pecans into cream cheese mixture. Spread onto bottom of crust. Continue as directed.

Preparation Time: 15 minutes
Refrigerating Time: 4 hours

Double Layer Pumpkin Pie

Layered Cranberry Cheesecake

Cheesecake dates back to Roman Empire days and still remains one of the most popular desserts of all time.

1 package (11.1 ounces) JELL-O No Bake Real Cheesecake
2 tablespoons sugar
⅓ cup butter or margarine, melted
1½ cups cold milk
½ cup whole berry cranberry sauce
¼ cup chopped walnuts, toasted

MIX crumbs, sugar and butter with fork in small bowl until crumbs are well moistened. Press firmly onto bottom of foil-lined 9-inch square pan.

BEAT milk and filling mix with electric mixer on low speed until well blended. Beat on medium speed 3 minutes. (Filling will be thick.) Spoon ½ of the filling over crust. Cover with cranberry sauce and walnuts. Top with remaining filling.

REFRIGERATE at least 1 hour. Garnish as desired.

Makes 9 servings

Preparation Time: 15 minutes
Refrigerating Time: 1 hour

JELL-O *Fun Facts*

Two fictional characters called Sammy, a boy, and Watson, his dog, introduced the concept of JELL-O Snacktivities in 1992. They were shown giving up fishing for an edible aquarium, spinning along on JELL-O pinwheels, and wolfing down Star Spangle Snacks on July 4th.

Luscious Lemon Poke Cake

This refreshingly moist cake has a surprise for all inside!

> 2 baked 8- or 9-inch round white cake
>   layers, cooled completely
> 2 cups boiling water
> 1 package (8-serving size) or 2 packages
>   (4-serving size) JELL-O Brand
>   Lemon Flavor Gelatin Dessert
> 1 tub (8 or 12 ounces)
>   COOL WHIP Whipped Topping,
>   thawed

PLACE cake layers, top sides up, in 2 clean 8- or 9-inch round cake pans. Pierce cake with large fork at ½-inch intervals.

STIR boiling water into gelatin in medium bowl at least 2 minutes until completely dissolved. Carefully pour 1 cup of the gelatin over 1 cake layer. Pour remaining gelatin over second cake layer. Refrigerate 3 hours.

DIP 1 cake pan in warm water 10 seconds; unmold onto serving plate. Spread with about 1 cup of the whipped topping. Unmold second cake layer; carefully place on first cake layer. Frost top and side of cake with remaining whipped topping.

REFRIGERATE at least 1 hour or until ready to serve. Decorate as desired.

Makes 12 servings

Preparation Time: 30 minutes
Refrigerating Time: 4 hours

1960

Graveyard Pudding Dessert

Even the ghosts will go for this!

An improved JELL-O instant pudding came upon the scene in 1969—a pudding so smooth and creamy that it was deemed suitable for pie filling, too. Its name was then changed to JELL-O Instant Pudding & Pie Filling.

3½ **cups cold milk**
2 **packages (4-serving size) JELL-O Chocolate Flavor Instant Pudding & Pie Filling**
1 **tub (12 ounces) COOL WHIP Whipped Topping, thawed**
1 **package (16 ounces) chocolate sandwich cookies, crushed**
Decorations: assorted rectangular-shaped sandwich cookies, decorator icings, candy corn and pumpkins

POUR milk into large bowl. Add pudding mixes. Beat with wire whisk or electric mixer on lowest speed 2 minutes or until blended. Gently stir in whipped topping and ½ of the crushed cookies. Spoon into 13×9-inch dish. Sprinkle with remaining crushed cookies.

REFRIGERATE 1 hour or until ready to serve. Decorate rectangular-shaped sandwich cookies with icings to make "tombstones." Stand tombstones on top of dessert with candies to resemble a graveyard.

Makes 15 servings

Preparation Time: 15 minutes
Refrigerating Time: 1 hour

JELL-O Fun Facts

In the late 1930's, the phrase "Look for the Big Red Letters on the Box" made its appearance in comic strip-type ads featuring Jack Benny and Mary Livingston.

Graveyard Pudding Dessert